Silence Severed to a Story Foretold

KAUSHIK TANEDAR

ISBN 979-8-88883-977-5

Contents

Contents

Poetry
కావ్యము

Short Story
చిన్నకథ

*Simpler hearts... stuck with the softer lyre of love.
Such pangs shall nature reveal for cheering light
across elysian lands.*

~ Kaushik

Poetic Philosophy

కవిత్వ తత్వశాస్త్రం

The Dimension of Philosophy

What is the dimension to philosophy?
Unlike any easily flowing thought, its dimension is a delicate thread.
Maybe it has a very distinct appearance,
A faint appearance of its being, with a shape, color of the skin, an idea of heartbeat, bob collared shirt, bell-bottom trousers, or even naked like the primeval man.
Stories of life are found in their very own philosophies,
On the lips you first kissed,
On the body you first laid heart on,
Within the poetic snuggle between the fingers laid across the bed,
With the emerging poetries puffing and cuddling across the layers of the skin.

You've immortalized her in your papers and the pencil was never tired,
When we were robbed of these ecstasies,
They weaken our trust, belief, and strength but with time and time alone.

It starts to embrace wisdom with an act of seeking profound sadness,
With a rush in blood to contemplate the creation and creator philosophically.

And the symphony sets its way in words penned or colors painted,
Maybe this is a dimension to the philosophy of universe,
To the ideology of meaning to think or simply just observe one's mind.

Art is not a monologue, it hands out a considerate dialogue with the deaf, dumb and inattentive.

The Conscious Act

Is love conscious?

When we speak of unconditional love, what are the
conditions we are aware of?
There are a million ways to understand it.

Why is it that it is as beautiful as a sunny day for
Shakespeare?
Why is it a form of strong expression for van Gogh?
Why is it a disaster for Nietzsche?

I have heard the world express it with a million flower
beds under the moonlight,
I have read the most profound works on it,
An elegant positivity, a clean soul, a divine creation of
the universe...

Like the land of heaven with fields of its own laws and
justice.

How do we define its beauty?
What do we know about it and how little have we
experienced it?

To some. Its passion, muse, a living piece of art, a philosophy to write on, poetry to narrate, a paradox to visit, a memory to feed.
In guilt or love to experience or experiment,

An act of romance, a wound with wisdom.

Love alone is a compelling story, two people in it are in conflict,
Love is a new color in you,
A field with gold,
A promise of misunderstood reality,
You see? Now, this is yet another form I am putting love into.

The night goes in for a whiskey on rocks by a silent river stream.

Jealousy

How do we define jealousy?

What is to call for an uneasy feeling?
In profound lights of the heart where sorrow or guilt or happiness is a perfect path to understand, but jealousy or envy share a very thin line of difference.
Would we be happy to witness our loved ones in great success?
How do we propose jealousy in connection with the beloved?

Yet again, what does love have to do? What does love do to us? What is love?
A different paradox, a different role, a different act, a pearl of different wisdom alltogether?

I guess it is an incomplete experience combined with the buds of love,
A belonging widely spread into the arms of seeking.

The sun goes down, night comes in,
We are not tired of the same old mind,
Reclined by the river light, we smoke the neon light,
A passing stream in darkness,
I am a man of dreams.

Moonshining down to the river,
With a form lurking under the street,
We hear it,
We feel it,
We seek it,
We belong to it.

With time, we are walking.
Our lives are changing with whiskey and wondering,
Our hearts are wandering,
Our dreams are crashing with a hand in hand.

With shoulders in vain and unpleasant seriousness in
a mortal dress and pity dressing gown.

Man

He was tired. The story hardly begun,
His shoulders are bare, a letter stood in his hand,
Eyes with brightened candles burned all night,
In a distance, the church bells tolled,
Grains of fear in him shook,
With nothing to celebrate... Gathered his feet and
rose.
dressed in a silver buttoned shirt and strolled through
the street, his honor was the front row.

She sees him with a thin empty hand,
Quietly greets her regards and kisses her man,
He sells his prayers and offers his heart,
For she's got another man.

A song of departure sang back in his heart.

Under the July sun, he hikes the woods and skies, sits
by its warmth and paints a lake.
Birds break a melody for the day,
Pain catches symphony under his breath,

For his chahat was his life, he was madly in love.

A perfect awful rain falls like the lawless crowd,

An anthem sings in his heart,
Every man in love has heard it,
With a bearing inconvenience and devotedly bitter cry
of despair,
Pain is a deserted island,
Sorrow is a dearest persuasion forced upon,
Forced upon?
A heartless legend of pity,
An unkind heaven with sudden anger and yielded
entreaty,
An uneasy shame within a heart.

The wiped eyes of a man are driven by compassion,
With arms wrapped about a shallow suffering,
A comeback that is fancy,
Wisdom like a finely aged wine, on throats that aren't
just one,
Stories written and flowers that are sealed,
Like the luminescent glow of a firefly,
A melodramatic charm sealed on the lips forever.

He becomes a passing river, with no sudden suspicion
by an ominous landscape.
A dry-eyed agony, calm nerves, and a steady voice.

He steps on the path with will cut in half,
Frowning a little, fainting a lot.

A tragic longing and a bittersweet laughing,

Twisted mind and shaking terror,
From self-control to longing relief.

Brandy and soda...

With coming time, his fears wither,
With seasons, reasons reign.

Love a man, don't punish.
You'll make a fool out of yourself.

In a thousand miles ahead, with a distant expression,
but distinctly to be seen... he designs his death.
His love will startle you and extend a little shiver!

You're a solitary creature...
He shines more than ever.

24 Oct 2021.

चाहत

Under an animate sun-speckled sky, she sat with the thick umber hair crossing her shoulders,
Like the whirls of fish in the lake acchoda,
Sipping by the sun's harmonious rays spying from the curtains,
With her meditative eyes and a romantic smile, she's a precious little thought.

Sloping fields and vaguely lit clouds in the background,
Peasants by the fields and fences stood certain.

I held the palette with suspender trousers, the red-roofed huts and trees with a variety of softer green appeared in the distance.

The winds calmly blew with an organic stillness,
And the pleasing colors of the blue-green assembled

She's like a young river gathered by flowers, Soft and lovely... yet painfully distant.
Her cheeks were often kissed,
Hair articulately clasped in my fingers when her caramel eyes danced merrily with mine,
Her voice... mild and mellow, like an enchanting field of flower beds.

In her oyster white cotton gown, she looked all sixteen. Shyly perching in the fragile green fields, she's a delight where darkness lost its thought.

She lay on the bed with a light shift,
Her arm lay across my chest in a sleepy murmur,
Whenever i kissed her, my eyes shut in a divine grip,
Our love was like drawing a tight clasp of medieval ruins with kings and kingdoms and ballads and dramas.

It made us strong and bold in love...
At her neck... he took a long softening breath.

Birth of Thoughts

A dull act of existence ran in the background,
I light the cancer stick and extend it to Iqbal.

Two cane chairs with a bowl and pitcher on a table alongside,
After a firm drag, he looks up at the royal blue-tinted sky,
Says, you know? All through our life we experience, feel, contemplate, and sometimes emit a tremendous amount of thoughts. Maybe a thousand years ago a thinker might have sent the same thoughts from exactly where we're sitting.
Maybe he looked up at the sky with the same confusion and questions for life.
Maybe he left them in the open sky before death shook his hand.
But, were the thoughts received by us? Or any in the past?
Are these thoughts immortal?
What could they look like if we could see?
A simple question of being able to receive someone's thoughts is profound to think of, isn't it?

Maybe it's a dance, a dance so slow and together.

Maybe the warm breath against our necks, slowly breaking the strings in our hearts.

With so much to say, so much to understand, and little less to give up,
Maybe, it is a new world altogether, a thin line between love and hate, a border between strange weather and a brave new world, a paradox that couldn't be seen, a perfect dimension to our imperfect naked minds.

An art with fascinating guideless unspoiled social affair,
A depth in literature and the glory of a poet,
A creation of heaven and hell with colored balloons,
A festival of love with ceremonies of philosophy.

Is Morality a Mortal Thought?

Is morality a mortal thought?

Let us consider the immortal walls of sorrow,
And that you and I share the same pathway in it, like
the street with a lamp.
The strange crowd of emotions sometimes belongs to
the lies.

If I give in to god, the ultimate divine and all-knowing,
the mortality of his morals must have stumbled upon
the creation typing this.

In the vivid void, of endless tragedies and trivialities
and luck, where does the border of existence lay?
This is an open book... To write and to read, to ignore
and to burn for warmth.

In love, in a happily accepted law and justice, where
does the sacred punishment survive?

To a primeval man, what was love?
What were morals?
Did he know he was mortal?
Did he understand what death does? Or what it was?
What gods did he discover?

What did the stars do to his nights?
What appreciation or fear did he share for a full moon?
And what was fear to him?
In the nights with the crescent moon, what understanding did he have for the missing light?
What was lust for him and how did he start to communicate with the divine if he found one.

To Vincent nature was god, to Nietzsche was god an idea? Kuvempu had his poems and Oscar with his strongest expression.

Yet today, truth is something we are trying to "understand"

So then, what human actions were cherished?
Maybe in the transcendental symphonies of a night, did a primitive man remember his yesterday and picture a tomorrow?
Whilst this pretense of the universe continued,
A spark of foolish pride and good deeds were found.

But for any primitive life, earth had put out a show, a confusingly strange one, an amusing blue of the day met the vermillion sea under the setting star.
A calming pulse settled with a song in the fields they lay,

A never before read book of hymns bloomed under this light, not just any but all moral and mortal hearts had witnessed this.

Dark clouds afloat the sky and rain falls for the divine,
The blue horizon and scarlet lake battlelines were sewn within his clasped hands,
With a deep sigh, he shuts his eyes for reasons to shut,
Dust of life grows into a fragile new plant, for morality to bloom or mortality to survive…

The creation and the creator.

Ignition

In the denser lands of pain, positivity loses its grounds
to smaller days.

Cave systems for care and affection, life in greater
towers.

Tiny winds and profound thoughts,
Hearing the unnatural songs from seven men,
The sprinkling leaves, chirping birds and rural fields,
morning melodies and the moment lost in time.

Exotic flowers, erotic pleasures, weaker bonds, tender
thoughts, trembling candles, dreamy nights with gods
out of sight.

A more particular harmony from the roots and woods,
complex particles of art under rivers. living, evolving,
dying and gracefully winning.

Like the blooming lotus of Shakuntala,
Ink dipped quill of Kalidasa,
Streaks of wet hair and the bare shoulders of Urvashi.

Symphony

A difficulty restlessly wandered,
I invited time with cries and cigarettes.

I have been painting in the fields,
I waited for the dust to settle down,
I did not even blink with a steady look of necessity.

Blackbirds gather for goodbyes,
Black brides walk through the fields.

Suspending a darling by the lake,
By the western river, I answered the calling of the tides,
The delicate sand and delusional laughter.

An outrageous thought restrained a cry.

Who is I?
Who is we?
A blank smile traveled by my lips,
With hope floating on my lids,
Wild storms scattering the sea,
Stutter passing through my voice,
Shadows of reality rattling in million more ways,

Madness changes in my wits with an absurd thought,
a brave illness, and a possible despair.
A confusing consciousness. . .

Kings of many lands judge another's crime, with
impatient concern, and calming fight.

My voice, cold and hard with no excitement for the
lonely night,
Galaxies and particles of charm peeping through the
sky,
An empty-headed illusion confused with a vulgar
scandal of grievance.

A lookout for sweet perfume in the single desert's
heat,
The intoxication of moon,
A lotus rose in my hand under the historical flicker of
the stars,
With an immobile gaze, I shrugged at last.

An instinctive desire hung in my dull red eyes,
Shadows were set free,
Sympathy calmly prayed a natural death.

Life blurted out from my delicate hands. . .

Tenderly a leaf fell upon his fallen heart.

What is Philosophy?

I have been meaning to tell you this, my friend,
When we look at things, events, situations in a deeper understanding, in their deeper interpretations and paradoxes, we tend to miss out on the certainty of these incidents.
Maybe for all you know, the world is meant to be as it is,
Maybe philosophy is a term that is widely agreed upon or coined by a thinker a thousand years ago,
With every contemplative understanding of an event, we ignore or tend to ignore the widely accepted comforting answer,
Comforting answer?
Maybe that is how the evolution of civilization and society understood it or accepted it.

What is philosophy then? Is it an expression to ignite the soul of a soulless thought?
In many possible ways of questioning, understanding, contemplating or internalising a thought as my guru tells me, is there a possibility for a profound path with a grip on thought and emotion?

Is the process of existence a calm and pleasant one?
Do we have the ability to see thoughts and events in their normal state?

What is normality then?
How thin is the border between sanity and insanity?

Is philosophy a songbird from the garden of heaven?
A dance?
A ballad?
A musical tragedy?
An epic?

When did it start and where does it end?

My understanding lays on the grounds where mind breaks the threshold of accepting what it sees and questions the birth of an emotion.
To me, it is a form of expression that has no rightful expression at all. With a way of balancing good and evil, it needs no answers.
You see? There are no answers in this cosmic dust, there are either pleasant or agreeable ways to understand anything.

One thinks, in an attempt to find answers... that the answers are mysterious like God's work.

With a nod, Iqbal speaks. Breaks free from a suitable silence and proceeds...

Kaushik,
My dear kaushik,

Philosophy is a way of life I enjoy.

In a word, when I'm riding my bike I care less about the taxes a firm collects, the restorations they need to do with passing time, or improvement in the next 5 or 10 years.

I just enjoy the road, I just enjoy the ride, sure... these thoughts come to me in one way or another. But the idea of having to think of its past, its evolution, and its conclusion gives me relief of finding an answer, or must I say an agreeable opinion?!?

The moment becomes a tranquil bliss, the question of someone a thousand years ago coining it as philosophy doesn't occur to me then but it does... with its own time and effort.

Is it really a philosophy or an agreeable name by the human race?

The thought of being able to think from the times of a primitive man is a form of philosophy yet again.

हमें और जीने की चाहत न होती
अगर तुम न होते

Like a needlecraft watched to its final progress,
Fascinating and slow. . .
Lovely neck, graceful hands, the slope of the shoulders,
with a perfect and imperfect battle in the heart.
An admiringly growing figure that's fresh and clean like a painting in process,
Her smooth skin like moisturized work of varnished portrait,
Summoning the west wind between her hair and neck,
A good flow of heartbeat slumbered under her soft breasts... with nipples plunged firmly beneath the white silk sarong.
Her shining chestnut hair and cheeks aglow with innocence.

He took her into his arms, they clung into a divine grip and kissed one another on the tender sweet lips,
A passionate love it was, they made love with fulfillment and supreme commitment,
With a shiver passing through them very joyously, sincerely, passionately within their heart, mind, soul, and body.
Heaven spread out between them like a work of Rembrandt.

For some, love was a casual act of consumption,
For a few, it was a deeply emotional and harmonious bending of mind.
A dimension of senses bringing life, goodness, and righteousness.
Love is like a seizure in the heart with an added burden,
Like the creation of a universe with its destruction and dance,
Love... is a companion to appreciate life,
Love is a garden of heaven with lakes and magnificent trees and tender plants embroidered with the fragrance of divine excitement and pleasure.

She put her face in the rain, a shivering chill passed through her freed arms...
An unusual affection, a scandalous wit, a sensuous chill, a mischievous excitement, a stage for conceived romantic dance passed through her soul.
Love, for her, was a flower on a tropical land with its own story to tell. But to him, it was a symphony of sharp instruments... a puncturing fusion of poetries and poems and poets between the battlefields and paradise walls.

Love was a charity offered to his trivial life. A road where seeds of delicate threads were sown.

Wisdom of Love

Thoughts are seasonal, sometimes mighty, sometimes
at ease with dignity.
A great awakening for the couple. . . it is a hymn book
full of ballads to sing.
A tune in discord.
People in love can hear to it with a silence at heart.

Love is a road with land on either side,
A thought that carries a forest to the left and rivers
on the right,
Like the devoted energies around the fire in the living
room,
The ghazals of Jagjit, the sweet buzz of the rain,
warmth in each other's bodies, and the beauty of
darkness.

A table stood, with a teapot and book of favorite
enemies,
Miserable prints of affection in mind, sorrow becomes
a cushion to sleep on.

Like a firefly with hypnotic noises, fancy fairylands of
happiness, mischievous murmurs, with tales to tell by
angels drunk.

What could we possibly feel?
What sentiments can we send?
Will they hear it in our voice?

Love is a jealous affection in a mighty 17-year-old,
With childish suffering and growing sympathy,
Love is a perfect reflection on transparent water,
Love is a vulnerable language with dense expression.

We suffer no surprise nor enjoy any,
A loyal porcupine with long-lasting pleasure,
A man is a man and a woman is a woman with their
stories wrapped under their feet,

The universality of wisdom to understand the nature
of the world and a man is a gentle dedication.
It is an attraction to adventure,
An attempt at exploration,
It is a compelling story.

The Deceiving Evening

A virgin sense of clouds, the deceiving evening.

Prospered beach by the feet, static energy walks alongside every being.

The evening's an honor, a goodbye bidding with sunset, a night for wet drinks and dreams...

This is the nonsense of life, an hour or two is how it is.
A lullaby to sing on the arms of saturn,
A taste very sweet for the lips of love,
A moment of freedom all over this world,
A bewildered reality for the chained.

People walk by, some with thoughts and some... thoughtful.
Some.. sitting under the glaring sun in an artistic assemblance.
This is the secret to life, a rare movement in these evenings.

People with loosened grips on the past, profoundly in love and delicate with diplomacy.

The dirty old road, hindering cold waves striking the flames,
Unalarmed noisy little poets,
Words rewritten and wounds revisited.

जब प्यार करे कोई

तो देखे केवल मन

A language enfolded and stitched in the human heart,
With an unconscious image till the day of existence.

Love is an exhibition of man's despair,
Love is a warmth in winter gripped by need,
Love is a rebel against living,
A Westwind towards the wetland,
Tears of lightened burden in an embracing pot,
Love is a perfection that merely strives,
Love is the queen of hearts like a finely aged wine,
Like the pearls shimmer on the slumbering tides.

Love must be protected, for it mustn't cripple.

Like the words of Glenn "You look in her eyes... the music begins to play"

Love is a night of fantasies,
For nightingales to sing and fireflies to swing,
For the woods to dance with the streams in trance.

Love is a part of one another,
For words to part and poems to form.

An alarm to remind the existence, a forbidden path towards freedom.

Our race has endured the gift to think,
To think is a profound experiment one can do,
An exploration to selfmade consciousness,
An attempt to touch imaginative realities,
A source to envision life beyond closed territories.

Letting life happen and making life happen has a difference,
Painting and writing are my two wonderful wives.
Why perhaps the world coined us "The tortured souls"?

Within the frame of human condition, the practice of denial and disbelief had endured a long long way.
Like love...
In love, one is capable of being combined with the spirits of the mind and realms of the soul. One needlessly conjures oneself up with disbelief and lack of trust.
An abundance of negativity... I may say.

Every practice of action in a philosophical, emotional, or poetic take exists in the great silence. We constantly exist in the vibrations of this vast universe in the great silence.

Things we talk of, think of, know of, read about, write about, contemplate with, deal with and conclude upon... exist in the great silence as the tiniest of tiniest specks of dust.

Our hearts and minds are intervened, like the sun and earth.
It is very delicate to notice that we are in constant consideration of directions from the mind.
Because we are taught "what" to think, not "how" to think.
In love...
One must always try and practise the emotion as naturally as it first occurred, with the same enthusiasm and spirit at heart and sincere thoughts at mind.

It is a compelling story, for we are in conflict.
Make it worth remembering.

The Soup of Love

He's barely home now, heard his terrible tales from bones in piles,
It's a mess, it is dark.
Tries to dig life from the dead.

The town's been old and lifeless, as lifeless as the wood that's been burnt.

He knelt and gripped the soil firmly, with all the strength left to leave the powdered face with the past. A trembling cry occupied his soar throat, kicking a jump from his stomach.

There's a leaf, a flower, a branch, and a plant under his blurred vision,
He's been loyal, he's been mocked, a pile of skirts and ugly thoughts turned to the corners of his mind.
His peals of laughter hung unignored as he stared straight into the soil,

A devastating effect gradually trapped his mind.

Life is like watching a soup boil, with a torrent of sobbing like the burning fire,

We do our best to serve it well.

In a stale perverted town with stammering peaceful years and storm-tossed weather, life is shaken with distraught. It sobs in unattempted efforts.

Cries and tears and sympathies for expensive pity,
We know what love is, under the autumn skies and starry nights it is no different to experience its craft.

Our lives are organic with a fact to die,
and beauty is a myth we carry in a lie.

The corners of our minds are natural and beautiful,
we only fall to rise back up.
Life grows from the dead, we scramble our art and write our love,
To eternity we take our tales.

Because life is well behaved and profoundly believed to grow out again,
It refreshes and recycles and births even better. Better than the soup we tasted.
Our tales would then be engraved on the rocks, life blooms into a more delicate leaflet, and then to a flower.

We pour our blood and sweat with efforts and nourishment into growth, we learn to grow where life is meant to grow.

We leave more behind when we walk to the stars.

In the wilderness, love is harmless. It grows in patterns and petals, in streams and cultures, in traditions and empires, in battles and ballads, in sensual practices and songs of quivered hymns, in a mother and her child, in a 17-year-old with his first handwritten letter, in unpredicted hearts and heartbroken artists.

And with chahat... one devotes the existence of life for love to birth even better and sweeter.

महाकाव्य

(MahaaKaavY)

I will recite to you a wholesome epic, tremble me with a foulsome tragedy.

I have attempted a pathetic, outraged letter with no warmth and sincere efforts.

My epic has a force to hold back, thoughts made for metal bars under a cabin in the winter woods,
I hath been listening intensely, moistened my lower lip, and shot a quick glance.
We communicated in silent signs.
In a firm expression, I began to count on my fingers.

My letters to you will remain in memory lane, my days pass with a good sense of absence. Next to me lay a pack of cigarettes in a decent manner.
My fantasies are yet again remembered and revisited,
I pull out a cigarette and light, reckoning my sustained days with a firm drag that paints warmth to the shivering cold harassing my skin.

An anxious heart, aching head, starving soul, and a disordered pale face reflected through the silver ashtray.

My head felt heavy to allow any music to slumber, I turn off the radio and sit in an idyllic meditative silence.

Abandoned tranquility swept through the mind, trapping a love story with pictures of a beautiful 24-year-old with fine dark hair, a sensitive face, and beautifully crafted brown eyes, Scarlet pink lips... when kissed, felt waves of sweetness come crashing into my chest. Between our skin, a fragrance stood twinkling through our nerves... like an extravagant wave crashing onto the sea rocks, my lips walked caressingly about her neck. We breathed through one another, through our sealed lips and gripping curves, through moving hips and erotic dots, through sensual love and exhausting sweat. As we fondled, she lay bare naked about me, surrendering me between her arms and warm breasts... a pleased twinkle always sparkled in her eyes, a spark like a shooting star would carry in the darkest of a night.

She lay snuggling in my arms by the half-closed curtains... under the low ceiling, the fireplace sent drifting sparks from the burning wood. The dark night admitted to her deep rhythmic slumber like a cradle under the warm quilt.
Her arm affectionately lay by the harmony of my chest.

An Embroidered Sculpting

Love is an art of sculpting,
We are the sculptors of our own legacies.
Of our own kings and queens, of our own reigns and monuments, of our own hustling battles and bloodshed glories.

Love is the art of sculpting from penning poems to singing ballads.

बिखरी जुल्फों ने सिखाई
मौसमों को शायरी

Every 17-year old kid had felt the possession of static energy with his first handwritten letter, with the first glimpse of his love, with her first word exchanged in love, with the first kiss they shared on the tender sweet lips...

We've made rhythmic and artistic tributes to these heartfelt feelings,
Shared our diction of heartbroken stories,
Wrote our message in the bottle,
Performed alongside our thoughts,
And admitted to it when it came as sweet as death.

Love's warmth has two sides...
An extra wood for the burning fire,
A drag on the tobacco to stir one's soul,
A sip on the spirit to sit and honor.

We are bound to an indulging logic. We grip to years of practice in loving, we either learn or simply misuse it. One must learn its essence, its script, its flavor of creation and destruction... Because love alone is the deepest fear one could discover.
It is an embroidery of a woolen rug, with its warmth... obligates us to its flesh and blood.

"Love is something totally new every day, but pleasure is not, pleasure has continuity. Love is always new, and therefore it is its own eternity."

~ J Krishnamurthi

In the fall, I hath chosen to learn its plot. I am a gentleman gathered by the fire to raise my spirit.

I've been its idyllic prey...

Winds began to change,
Solace stood last in the lane,
A promise came to visit,
I love as much as you shall sometimes regret it.

స్వర మాధుర్యం

(Melody)

The saddening dust from the unhappy clouds settles in,
We then seek the truth and discover the universe within,
We relate our stories to one another and see if we share more in common,
We search for life in other forms,
We search for love in other conditions.

We read familiar and similar tragedies with melancholic songs,
The tunes stay on repeat.

Dimly lit doubts are never too late,
Existence seems unlikely,
We rule out the possibilities and misunderstand reality.

We fail to embrace unpredictability, unlike nature at its best with every season and storm.
We come in many colors and forms, we adapt red for love,
We're connected.

Our hearts may appear dead for thousands of years,
Then, suddenly spring to life.
Life evolves in these wars, pain is a battle after all.

The world is a secret oasis,
A beautiful hideout for life,
Poetry, philosophy, romance, art, and love survive on
the deadliest surfaces possible.

Profound Women

Why is a woman profound?

She possesses energy, a quest for generations to ask,
Somehow, she is the flame.

A mixture of tunes the great silence held within,
A symphony our ears failed to listen,
A history of work the historians failed to study,
Poetry the poets lived for, with more commitment
and sincerity.

We have the honor of her love, we've had the honor of
her leaving,
She wasn't a coward's explanation, she was never a
prepared occasion.

New forms of cosmic dust are our thoughts of her
excellence.

Beauty is not what makes a woman,
The world wouldn't see a million poets and marvelous
artists without women in their lives.

Poetry

కావ్యము

The Velvet Candlelight

The room is comfortably quiet,

A serene scene runs across the verandah,
And whistling winds over the bending mist,
Ascending steps to a room on the distant shore,
Amidst the barren isle, thou art seen to smile.

Mellow sings the radio on freshening breast,
Divided by the dark blue brief,
A rolling sun parts the shore of pain,
An old wrecked chair and a heart to admire,
With a bowl of tempest's past.

He leans on her bending hair,
She walks in all charms in a white silk sarong.

The smooth silk generously lays on her nipples, revealing the art and arousal from her softly moving breasts.

He rose, slowly moved his fingers through her hair, and kissed her underlips,
Gropes her hips and rubs into her, with a moving romance on her neck, her sturdy neck... Her slender hands and thighs move harmoniously like the winds

of wild west end. A mass of freely flowing hair, caramel brown eyes, soft rose like sweet lips.

At the kitchen table, their romance became a blunt pencil sketch,
A million thresholds broke loose in their hearts.
They sipped a glass of wine each, allowing their souls to slave for pleasure.

The depth and despair, a story of perplexed odds and pleased evens with glory and greatness and madness.

Her being is like the grace of the sun between the fields of grape,
Like the characters in populated pictures and figures in renaissance landscapes.

An act of fragment love affair plunging into a rich human bondage.

Anthem

In the light of every heart, a hill was ascended,
Paths were discovered and melodies were hummed,
Their chapters were read by the rituals in the night
desert and pages... burnt with no desire.

Miracles have happened,
Lovers were married,
Hearts lost order,
But in the cave of every heart, an anthem was heard,
A profound prayer was offered where belief and
disbelief clashed.

The sculpted beauties walked the land without a piece
of shelter,
With time, discovered the stars and moon,
Hunger crossed our hearts with lifelines cut in half,
What joy we had?
What desires did we wear?
We're left to the universe to witness now.
We're talking to fire, there are no lonesome fights
In the blink of an eye, we'd be gone.

A child in our skin
His humor bled too much
And the darkness with an empty smile.

Do we sense our eyes now? They're barely proud
We had our thoughts with thresholds for light.

We're choking to death
We're startled and trapped
With enough time and unholy words.

We barely walk in the fields of barley
The price is dark with pride.

Let's take the hill while the heart is still brave
And leave the fights for cultures to fire.

हारमोनियम

(Harmonium)

The clarinets are dim,
With wrinkled wings and wretched marks.

A boat's wrecked,
Sea's blue,
Night breaks in with the sinking sun.

Belts and boots march towards the bar,
Tables and mugs clink in cheers,
With a longing in dreams,
Spurring flames and burning themes.

He stood with will, on the edge of a hill,
A soar scream under the blazing thunder,
Music slipping from the shameless shoulder.

Ballad

I make ballads,
I write pretty lines for pretty princesses across the
street.

My love is for a penny on the sheet,
I'm a woodpecker pecking words for a phony,
Out of the jungle jails and river lawns.

I write what I see, with confessions and sins in the sea.

I keep the demons very dear, there's nothing like gin
and places a man's heart been.

We come rattling and rolling like couples,
With hanging knives and coffins to cry.

Some are left alone,
Some are gathered,
Some honey and brandy will set the fire.

The schools are full with fine fellows,
With a hooker set up her shop across,
They turn in their sorrows,
She sits right over the drunk,
Serves right at their nose.

At the Gate of Eternity

Between love and hate, there's a thin line of loss,
You see? Sometimes the taste of a fruit, fragrance of a book, aroma of a dish, and memories of a road can take you back to nostalgia.
The memories may not always serve the best of laughter and joy, maybe not a sweet one but something very very bitter.

Having to acknowledge loss by any such experience comes from a very sincere and honest story of love.
These wars are immortal, Pain weakens us bit by bit, day by day, month by month, and year by year.
Such loss of tranquility and trust at heart is one of the greatest disasters any of us could experience.

Human bondage must lift off when a day ends, it must possess a beauty when night falls with studded stars, seascapes, hills nearing the moon, pleasant winds, and dramatic sitcoms.
All we need is a hand to hold us close so that we lay snuggling and a heart that listens, kisses and nurtures our soul.

A promising love to eternity.

That alone is god, keep your practices honest and the universe will be proud of your existence. Afterall, you are its dearest child.

Divine Tragedy

A love that is young finds its run with oceans crossed,
Miles to drive with mellow lines,

Visible wounds on repeat,
A heart with defeat.

The night is slow for wretched sex on repeat,
Singing words and scavengers on thee.

A constant guess the heart is meant to keep.

A thought on glue,
Confined to you.

Heart on coal,
Melody and tragedy,
Defining defeat.

An Absent Sweetness

My brother... my sister... did you march through the
border of life?
Have the papers made you cry?
Did the love letters die?

With a wound that's wise and wisdom with wine.

The line's here to depart,
Smile in your defeat,
Let the wider mile repeat.

Soul

ఆత్మ

I sat and gazed vacantly at the floor, my silence seemed
to nervously narrate a thought. With not a word put
out, a definite discomfort absorbed the room,
A bad dream, a bad purpose on hold.

"Oh dear"... now and then I murmured... Little after
little my voice died in a whisper.
Clasping my shoulders, I thought... how strangely we
are made!
In a low light, I kneeled with a rigid heart which I
fondled lovingly,
With a damaged cassette on loop, I put on a pale face
and rose hesitatingly.

A penned speech laid in the paper.

I hurried through the deserted streets, a coffin nail
firmly hung between my lips with a thick smoke
leaving me in temptation.

On a hill, women danced around the wishing well.
Faces painted with adinkra symbols by the gloating
flame.

The curves in yellow ochre aroused every possible temptation,
Awakening a petrified shadow and an artificial illusion.

In the dark corners, the designs of pilgrimages stood across the whole village.

Town

The town chained an old man,
Does love exist alongside hate?
Does it?

I,
Write.
I write with anger choking my throat,
With desire disguised as a slave,
With words put out in hunger,
With a soul starving,
Trying,
Trying to feed a fire in the temple.

The town chained an old man,
The old man needs a glass of rum.

A promise of nothing,
A love to fear,
A wife to love,
A sensation of contempt,
A lavish regret,
A shattered king,
A touch of the trembling hand,
A little laugh,
A heavy chest,

A hold on tears,
A pull on her hand, not letting her go but holding her close,
Close to her eyes, breathing by the neck, pressing by her breasts, and looking straight into her eyes.

He locked the door.

The Painted Hill

The winds with rich voices gathered,
The petals of a rose, painters, paints, bread and butter,
birds and barrels.

Confusedly smiling, he drew a long sigh under the currents of the sky and beams from the sun itself. A sensible silence gathered on his skin as he remembered his repulsive urge to kiss her.

His heart then sank.
From danger, it rose and it rose and it rose...

A strangely unusual picture appeared on the hill, a sinister wind delayed the storm.
His eyes!! bloodshot red, embellished a sketch and his head tormented fiercely as an unfurled stillness rose from the territory.
A trace of irritation moved in his voice when an acrid smell quickly kissed his nose. A tenderly fragile butterfly flew in a dance with a fruity floral fragrance in an attempt to seduce its love. His eyes twinkled, lips broke into a wide smile...
He was a damned fool,
A damned fool.

From this natural shock, he discovers his delicate heart, leans back on the sweet grass, rests the sketch and so does his eyes.
Remembers his dearest Kishore Kumar's **"Pal pal dil ke paas"**

And to think of words, of love, of poetry, and of death... he laughs.
More madly in love and more delicately than ever... a teardrop descends from his eye, Its gleam radiated like the very pearl of an angel perished from heaven itself and kissed the soil with a faint sound of chahat.

15 Oct 2021.

By Thy Mind

Sounding quite silly, mind goes under a pressure.

A damaged dance glances with a word, a letter perhaps.

His good looking charm, delicate nose, straight chin,
perfect brows and flawless hair.
He looks handsome.

A devastating past he couldn't change.

Keeping a difficult movement at heart, he gathers to
talk with his mother.
Realises how strange the possible time was,
November was cold, he'd warm himself with a glass of
rum.

He sips a sip with a sarcastic smirk on his face,
He thinks of an unhappy disability.

Life did not withstand his good manners or raging
handsome face,
In a caressing and deep affectionate voice he pulled
himself together.

A delightful expression in his sparkling blue eyes
appeared,
His evidently pleasant soul persuaded his tender
disposition in the heart.

With every self conscious mistake, it promised to
return again.
His curly moustache, long thick hair, teary eyes gave
an impression of beautifully put work of a painted
portrait.

The cuffs on his hands were amused to see her,
The affection and love confused and bewildered him.

He has been in love before, he has always been there,
he never broke the connection.

He knew what he knew, like a summer sun by the long
seascape.

Love is a perfect tool to break the madmen loose,
A charming fool is like a rosebud on the road.

The Afternoon

The striking sun came down an effortless afternoon,
Life longed under the july's sun.

Hefty voices and hammering noises settled in the port,
Dishonest applause, echoing voices, easy laughter,
sultry land, crowded clouds and frozen fields.

A ghastly painful silence shielded his face.

Summer nights of unused lives,
Harps partially broke and eyes partially wiped.

The still soil and strength disguised into temptation.

Persuading tunes of a marimba mounted the shoulders
of a pale angel.

Lighting a cigarette he calmly glanced at the wandering
spirits.

Spirits of imprisoned lives, of poor ones, of buds, of
powerful and unethical ones.

An august summer night with the singing radio, he stares at the spiked fence carefully covering the garden like a castle's high walling.

Kids in starched white and blue uniform, sketching the immersed
Scene in their books,
An outdoor that is fascinating and romanticizing i must say.

In his thoughts, she appears like the polished shimmer of the sea,
A female figure proportioned with the subtle shaped breasts, brilliantly knit hair, authentic eyes, rough lines of sketch appear on her waist as she walks.

She was a forbidden cup of criticism for critics to pen upon.

She was a painter's eye,
Like the fine burgundy wine from a vineyard.
Her nostalgic eyes, slim young body, glint in the skin, and the subtle lines on her neck.

A Painter's Melodeon

A faint shrug reached her shoulders, a warm smile appeared.
He was faithful to her,
He was a gentleman.

She was a good deal of godly charm,
There was nothing to make her pretty,
Prettier she was, and required no other foolish lies to dress her.

Her pleasant voice, casual manner, politeness, compassion as a painter's wife shaped a history to their art,
This is history for poets to sing.

He shook to a sweet little pain in his chest,
It was natural enough with no story to tell.
Looking severe he turned to the dark corners of the room,
A fine line of melody sang,
The melodies of the past.

Her prominent cheeks, her finely crafted caramel brown eyes, butter like yellow face, lustrously polished black hair, well shaped magnetic charm with her promising love and merciless nagging wrapped him in a sparkling poetry.

They were not strangers to seductive mornings, their love lived through small dinners, admirable talks with lasting affection.
 Loving her was his noble practise, a possession his heart had endured with a glory.

A darkness went by with the passing hour, an emotional turbulance stirred all feelings of fear and loss, every possible calmer moment cradled his tears around the cheek.
Her beautiful eyes dazzled like dewy ponds under the green nightscape, like the dreamy sun engaging its light with the young widowed soil.

The night rhythmically composed itself, for he could sit and watch to confess by the candlelight. At first, he was delighted to think of her. He felt his own sufficient longing with no reason to contend. An acquaintance of blush slightly appeared on his face with the thought. He was his own author and composer.

A passionately sentimental love story he wrote...
She now belonged to his pen, and he, to her story.

Blue Road

Trapped at the blue road,
I am shot in the leg, for i need to leave,
Chained to my ribs and killed on the field.

Dogs of death leave me be.

I held to the gate and rose,
Keys at the back door left me be.

On an early morning, i sat and drank two jars of rum,
And the love drained.

I then walked the road less walked, climbed a truck
with my old bag, eyes tiring with shiver beating upside
down,
With a prayer on the lips and some extra blessings,
Not the best ones yet.

I lashed at the desert's sun and remembered what my
father,
Be true to yourself and let the heart sink into another
ocean.

Freedom with a flaw...

With my eyes closed and no self improvement for philosophy,
I did my best with a voice holding back again,
Crossroads at the sick end won't let a dream in mud.

With every beat in the heart, heaven's tides crashed on the grave,
The moon is now in the dark holding a pale angel.

My letters float in an abyss with roses and darkness in every hand.

She lays on my chest, runs her fingers through my hair and wonders if I ever loved her.

Comes to know that I have been dead.

Seductive Cloud

An appealing smile flushed.
We preserve color, character, place, person, sentiments, time and photographs of our beloved.
Love is an act of cherish, a practice of a very profound drama, an epic tale that intervenes with the roots of our hearts.
There's a battle within love and agony.

One must begin to recognise love as an individual art, and their artists...different from others with a contained glory of honest practice.

The evenings are calm and dramatic with scenes of cradling breeze.
Something about the valley, flight of birds, humble breeze, warm sun, sweet grass above the flowery renaissance land.

Tears parted from our lids, the moon rose hushed.
A poetic maze with a persuasion, he fondles his heart and shuts his eye,
He perceived their clasping hands and blush under the blanket,
Her mystic glittering eyes appeared with the fading illusions of the cosmos.

The mist of seductive cloud gripped a soul,
An unawakened cry glittered by his lashes,
The smell of her neck permeated his body,
Patience punctured under the roof of his chest.

Like Michelangelo's expression of high renaissance. . . a
divine depiction, connection, myth and a religious vision.
The serene colors and fascinating details.

The Mist of Despair

The morning drew, sun touched the mist and shone its golden light on the river.
Piercing all the way to the eyes,
Like being touched by a magic wand,
Like the work of a magician with the fragments of spells and flowing colors.
Blooming vastly here and there by the yellow rays like yellow ochre,
The twinkling tips of grass,
An extravagant pattern with unimaginable richness.

The sky stands like a fortress where no man or god could enter, like the fabric of a dream no human hands could ever create.

Tears ran down his face as he gazed,
With hands tightly clasped at his chest,
A pure spirit broke from his soul.

The mighty dawn had passed the massive darkness,
Vaguely remembering the incidents sent a shiver down her spine.

A hundredth day. . . a hundredth hour. . .

An enough human pity to seduce the heart,
A shrewd coldness cleansed their hearts,
Behind the charming eyes were the words that sounded silly,
Love surely is an attractive trait for humanity.

Hearts are hungry for flattery,
Life pushes us to prove cleverness and stupidity,
Passion kisses our lips with a childlike affection,
Life becomes less tragic to cry in sleep,
A careless laugh, merry little eyes and cynical curiosity.

With an eccentric amusement to freedom, our lives slip into bizarre adventures,
Beneath the titanium white sky was laid an ominous land by the mother nature's guiding hand,
Painted hills, fantastic nature, violent skies, green heads of trees, water buffaloes, grateful gods and a happy dog.
Nature was at its most effective pose.

Life is a pretty good idea to live, with harsh compassion for whiskey and soda
A deadly persuasion for wisdom with grinning laughter and trembling patience.

Life is a sustained symphony of hidden instruments with delicate hands,
Life has a striking beauty.

Obedience to humanity and compassion,
An attempt at art and literature,
A remembrance of a young sun and fondling moon.

Still

చలింపని

We gripped to ecstasy between our naked thrill,
A satisfaction still and full.

Gentle lovers that we are, our flames burn to miles
that could carry our poems afar,
Few hours... a few days... few years... that i keep
walking.

Our stories have a trace, no one knows our place,
The answers are far, letters settle on the rocks.

Dancing in the sun and the rain,
Kissing by the big river.

Glory

కీర్తి

A melodic trance settles by the pleasant fields,
Peasants and birds chirping in an audible distance,
Winds rise and recede in a crashing manner,
Wild rabbits and dogs slumber under the fresh foggy morning.

The colors are rich with an aged tenderness and glow,
They hum to awaken with subtle consciousness.

The sun... Earth's distant lover held his light.
For one thing or another, birth flickers in the blooming plants,
With nurturing eyes and affectionate intimacy.

Creation is divine for the creator be devoted.

The red river valleys, aromas in air, ancient forests
and songs of gandharvas heard by poets at ganga.

The Burgundy Dream

The December snow drifted, a beam from the moon admitted through the open curtains. She lay snuggling in the middle of the bed with a body like the petals of tulips.
A rhythmic chorus blew the clouds apart on the lonely sea... the grains on her affectionate shoulder sailed cradled with a harmony of enigmatic smoke.
A blue green flame stood idyllic on the candle I held, I stood by the books she had been reading before the sleep romanced with her.

A magnificent blending of spiritual ecstasy moved through her eyes as she moved next to my vacant hand, multiplied with intensity a profoundly stirring physical passion swept through my tender artistic heart.

To our left, a storm gently and slowly touched the shore, like an anchor fell thudding on the moist land, her heart dropped under the moist lids,
I dearly endured her hand in a promising grip.

She was a work of art to persuade the passion of an artist, an exuberant section of her hair passed through the curvy and slim waist line. A beam of mellow light stood enchanted with the departing moon.

She is the essence for flowers to bloom, stars that become visible with night, sun that descends into the sea and a compassionate impression of sparkling beauty in her bare body.

At my sight, she stood in a burgundy scarlet white gown that drew through her cleavage like the crescent moon under the autumn night.

She's like a painting formed by michelangelo,
Her perfectly proportioned body shone like the reddish tones of the birthing land,
As she descended the stairs of heaven, gentle breeze and love gods looked up to witness the divine creation.

In through her deep cleavage a shimmering blue sapphire pendant was hung. She possessed a knowledge of magical prowess, she revealed herself into a perfumed spring.

Here I stood... shivering like the flickering flame in a lamp,
Like the drained wick clouded by the damp dark smoke,
With a romance that the world loves from afar.

You held out a hand, and a strange music held a soar taste of radiance upon my eyelids.

Resplendent face... shied away oh mi heart at thee... ah... fairest dream!! Thine beauty maketh mine spirits stir.

Disgust

Old town i wandered with a dissolution in you,
I walk with the dirty paths, eyeing the ridicules of
smokers and drunkards.

Holding their tongues between fingers and pleading
men to fuck,
Balanced on hungover heads and tender on helpless
hearts.

I gather not a flower for thee,
By means of growth and beauty, thy fragrance grieves
for death in thee.

The great walls, territories of relief, humble
philosophies, ballads of battles, prisons of confession
and principles of lust.
Practicing until the religion maketh you its slave.

I will bring thee the flowers from garden of eden,
Romantics from Rome and secrets from scotch.

Thy will walk with flowers held in hand and slaughter
them all,
For thy is not divine for the beauty thee heart secan.

Short Story

చిన్న కథ

చిత్రకారుడు

The Painter

Mankind belonged to a land of great noble expression.

In its vastness with a warm heart, it braced all the affections and earnest living.

Secrets the land shared, the terror it beheld, faith and hope it endured, and horrors it had seen from every little room.

The times are now quite far to gather any precision on the tragedy that occurred several years ago...

"Perhaps, you may listen to it."

One afternoon, the sun stood still and for miles the day spread with sunshine, its brightened colors perfectly radiated the sky. The spacious valleys with sheep spread among, fields of gold across perfectly crafted lofty mountains, families and huts, and cattle, children with indistinct voices of joy and laughter that seemed to be positively alive.

And with all, people seemed to share a loving familiarity with one another.

Nature was in her finest mood of playfulness...

Andhaka was born in *Ayyavari Palli,*

He grew up with a generous excitement in assisting and helping his mother around.

Andhaka was intelligent and had a kind smile and tender simplicity. Besides, he shared a peculiar portion of his love for art.

With time aging to its wrinkles, his aspects of life became responsive.

Andhaka developed a sense of art in fables, he often sketched and painted mythical stories resembling parietal art. He carefully crafted tales in his paintings with a sense of enchantment and composition.

With time, Andhaka was deeply stirred by the idea of people assuming control over their emotions. His unspoken words searched for lips sealed. He was drawn to blood, fancying its appearance and taste. He developed a sense of lust towards his new emotions and beheld them with a fascinating pleasure.

Beneficence had left his body.

Being shrewd and active, he never permitted anyone to know he was a painter. His work made it look far more gorgeous than the subject.

By the time Andhaka turned 27, he began Plein-air and loved nature in a more affectionate way. To him, it offered innocence and freshness in both good and evil manner, like the prey and predator, villain and victim.

One evening, there was excitement all over the village, strangers appeared by the lake, as the red trails of the setting sun were polishing the dim-lit sky.

Andhaka rambled over to the west corner of the valley for a shade to rest his easel and paint, in a soft khadi kurta with a jute bag strapped alongside.

In due time, from amongst the leaves and the picturesque barks of the trees, a crystal bend of light could be seen resting from the descending sun.

A faint motion of affection came to him and stirred a painful memory in his eyes, a naturally shattered heart endorsed pain and pleasure in the fields and around.

He'd learned to love nature more, all the less. A deep hum of **Jagjit ji**'s *"Yaad nahin kya kya dekha tha"* bled from his lips.

About this time, by the late hours of the night, when shoulders of labor stretched a heartful slumber across the valley... Andhaka sat in his richly ornamented portico and watched the moon infuse its beam of illuminating tenderness.

The night seemed afloat in harmonious symphony. The mountain streams murmured, winds whispered among the woods for an idle tale to begin...

The world had to wait, to see what held this man with such rage.

Andhaka was filled with a still thought, sipping on scotch with his lustrous black hair flowing to shoulder length, perfectly parted in the center to a sharp grip standing still in his forbidden eyes behind the thin-rimmed spectacles sitting on his straight nose.

Gazing up at the village with an eager smirk, Andhaka grabbed his paints, brushes, easel, fish knife, an ax, a screwdriver, and a hammer into a thick rugged bag and began to pace out, quick like a predator.

The path lay before him now, a rumbling of wheels approached in the distance as he walked unnoticed in the darkened corners of the winding road.

A perplexed stretch of glare from the moon faintly painted the wet road, Andhaka's silhouette flickered in a dramatic manner by the mist.

Here he came...

There chanced to be a cottage by the riverbank, surrounded by wooden fences.

Seizing the opportunity, Andhaka slipped in quiet and quick.

The room's lustreless light flickered from a candle placed by a radio. The floor was made of variegated wood which appeared very old with irregular patches. Andhaka calmly moved in a stealthy manner with his right arm tightly gripping an ax, the room was quiet with a mysterious doom. A lofty door stood half open and a faint beam of light rolled out, for the gleam appeared certain beneath his eyelids... There was someone in the room!!

Andhaka thrust in, and within appeared a little woman, with skin as yellow as the burning candle next to the teapot, her radiant skin glistened and at once everything changed into a screaming voice that blared into his senses.

Her sharp eyes came locked with the weapon Andhaka had already launched right into her face, and in a moment... a crackling shrill sound of the impact vented with blood spurting out! Andhaka relaunched the weapon with incensed rage and speed!! The blade landed straight into the right eye, slicing it, splitting the head in two, and in a lifeless motion fell her body softly, thudding the wooden floor beneath. Standing with a scornful stare, Andhaka moved towards an inner room.

His patience had not had its meal yet. He turned around and two small kids about 6 and 10 years old appeared to be tucked in a small bed. Andhaka calmly withdrew the hammer out of his bag. He moved in silence, and an instant later, charged at their heads. The same striking sound vented out but it felt more tender, the kids gasped in a moment of pain and a thin sharp voice puffed out from their mouths. Their eyes… half-open. face and head, dissected!

An undeniable horror swept across the floor, the candlelight flickered mirroring its anxious panic on the gushing blood. The room became serenly quiet, only Andhaka's heart thumped in his ears! He now breathed in his low-pitched pleasure, slowly transcending with the flow of his thoughts.

Time seemed to move in an infusing manner, a divine satisfaction illuminated in his eyes.

Old Blood and Hunger himself… He knew not that thence would come better pleasure than could be learned from books.

As a soldier blazing on the battlefield, Andhaka licks the blood off his arms, savors, and in a hallucinating voice… "And why not? I am a man of taste, beyond a doubt!!"

All three bodies lay still, indeed, looked like a crowd that's testified.

Andhaka mirrored himself as a man with a character of art, he learnt no great art, nor hung one. Now, with his habitual breadth of view, remembers his conviction. Remembers to bless the bodies.

He drags the bodies into the common room and begins to search for a blade in his bag. He was ready for the world to acknowledge his brilliance in photographs, and reports about the incident in the newspapers. Contented with eyes fixed like a stone, he carefully peels the skin off the bodies, like a craftsman of death. After a great deal of work, he now completely deprived the bodies of any skin. Andhaka was beaten and worn out of patience, his bloody weapon reminds him of the inscrutable wisdom he beheld.

Enrobing himself in their blood and skin, Andhaka now danced and rumbled lines of eloquent poetry...

With a little time to cool, he was ready enough to do what must come next.

He reached into the bag and grabbed his materials, a 24x30 wooden frame, paints, palette, nails, and a surgical suture.

Like a poet well versed with his lines and a painter well equipped with strokes.

His killings were countless, a mind-bending horror and a fascination he shared for blood and art.

Andhaka began to stitch the shreds of skin together and nailed them into the wooden frame.

Now came one of the most meditative movements for him…

24x30 inches! "What a beautiful size for a brilliant work of art to sit and honor," he thought…

With enthusiasm serving in its finest joys…

Andhaka began to paint, like an illustrious commander whose tranquility was persuaded by the thrust of pleasure, to transmit the grand expression of a divine sympathy, to illuminate the ethereal spirits of the mountains, to marvelously craft the deep caverns of time on the radiance of freshly shredded skin.

He had imagined that this was his method of blessing mankind in a mood of poetic faith.

His mind is his pen, sailing straight to the horizon, with an eloquent sense of drama for life. It was an instrument that sometimes warbled the sweetest songs.

"Is not I worthy to resemble thee?"

He kept his hand continually moving, the brush confidingly made its strokes and went forth, his spirit endowed with nothing but truest truth. Bitterness bespoke in him as if Satan conversed with a horrific blaze.

He painted an unpardonable tale, to evoke an image that could neither be forgotten nor forgiven.

He paints the event of the murder!

Making himself home, Andhaka sat on a log of wood and lit a cigarette, pulled a firm drag... A slow and torpid feeling began to kick in, with his grizzled hair hanging about in sweat, his eyes deeply sunken towards the thin framed painting standing across the bodies.

As he stared in amazement... calmly... a slow heavy laughter in a childlike manner ascended its pitch in an evil modulation... an overjoyed laugh burst forth, a laugh as appropriate as a fearful death reverberated around the night.

Gazing into the hallow prison house, regardless of the fierce murder that reddened upon his face, he rose from the log, flung open the door, and exited.

Little did the village suspect this strange guest on a purpose, if not to evoke love, at least to plunge a murderous pleasure, thus vanish from the sight of man.

Perhaps the night had a mysterious doom, the flickering distant lights of the sleeping village, dimly radiant stars, lonesome winds, and the crescent moon.

A faint sweet scent pulled up from the woods.

At the hour of the sunrise, life seemed to follow its frequent custom around the village. The open air slumbered, inhabitants of life seemed to walk with farms arm in arm, and poets of the land began their songs for the first light.

A faint voice of a bird gently swept around the valley of waking.

And at a distance, but distinctly to be seen… appeared the rays of sun harmonized with life. Andhaka had finished his work of art and left the canvas standing still next to the horrifying event. The bodies remained untouched and unbothered for two days until the distinct odors of stale smell rose up around the neighboring huts.

Fear not because I open the door, I do but act by old custom.

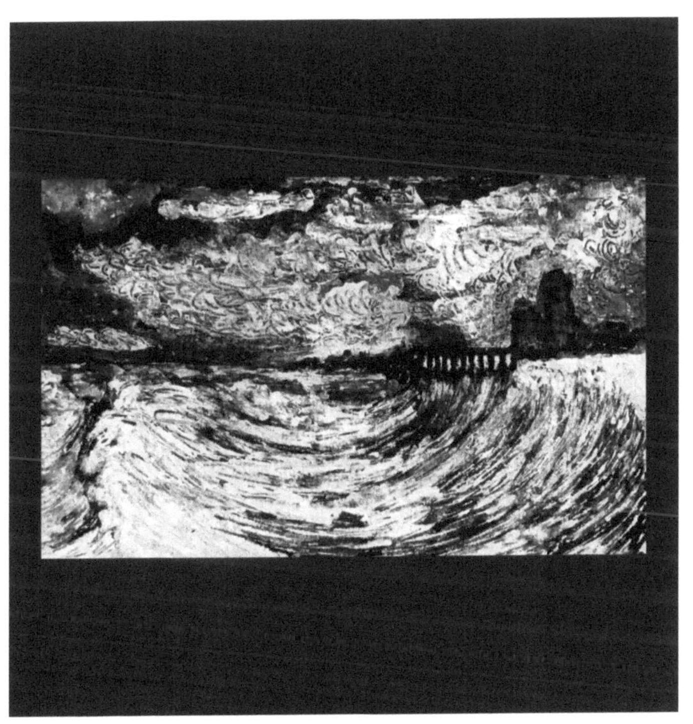

Tales of Idle Symphonies

And I walked,
I greet with no greed.

For every god and his hill,
Every man and his land,
Every place and its tale… had heard the songs of love.
Had touched the depths of one and clasped tears in rain.

For it is a path to truth
It is the truth.

~ Whiskey on rocks.

At heart's finest... an enchanting symphony arose

I cannot dream nor tell, must i no more avow?

My truth shall meet the gaze of a stranger's eye.
For the wandering thought leaves thee the nearer i
beheld.

~ Whiskey on rocks.

At every settling hour and a subtle
 minute... your scent dwells up in my heart.

Consuming its darkened chambers to leave
my feet in fleet.

Your smile... ascends in the wonders to see,
And words to seal.

~ **The portrait of a young lotus**

Leave my loneliness uncultured,
For death must find its wings to set the birds on feet.

Farther... the truth stood.

Push my heart onto a rose's thorn,
It will bleed with pride,
As white will stream red,
Thy heart shall never remain fed.

~ Nightingale

Grace...
Beams from the distant sun swept through the
wilderness.

Advanced by the sight of the horizon, the shades of
dusk arrived.

By the borders of a pond,
Sat the triumphs of thy agony.

In gaze... her lovely eyes tinkled,
Like two stars exchanging stony glances.

~ To remain thine.

I paint, to utter torment in every stroke.
Its literature devours me, savours my soul and
 imprisons the very trails of poetry.

~ Andhaka

Details that define art...
It is but the insignificant depth mind leaps onto,

A darkness that helps light stand out,
So be it art.

~ Agony

To set a heart on fire, one needn't express much desire. The evil strikes within first… later, extendes its hand for an enormous pang.

In other sense, to set a knee on soil and hold a hand for truth… one must burn with desire as red as rose.

To find such companion is to find true love. Because it needn't express grief of imperfection or efforts of involvement.

All it needs is confidence, then comes friendship.

And if you shall cherish it? So shall love nurture you.

~ Tickle.

9 798888 839775